Numbers and the Number System

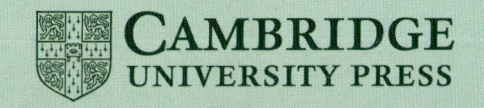

3

CAMBRIDGE UNIVERSITY PRESS

PUBLISHED BY THE PRESS SYNDICATE OF THE UNIVERSITY OF CAMBRIDGE
The Pitt Building, Trumpington Street, Cambridge, United Kingdom

CAMBRIDGE UNIVERSITY PRESS
The Edinburgh Building, Cambridge CB2 2RU, UK   http://www.cup.cam.ac.uk
40 West 20th Street, New York, NY 10011–4211, USA   http://www.cup.org
10 Stamford Road, Oakleigh, Melbourne 3166, Australia
Ruiz de Alarcón 13, 28014 Madrid, Spain

© Cambridge University Press 2000

First published 2000

Printed in the United Kingdom at the University Press, Cambridge

Typefaces Frutiger, Swift   *System* QuarkXPress 4.03

A catalogue record for this book is available from the British Library

ISBN 0 521 78456 5 paperback

General editors for Cambridge Mathematics Direct
Sandy Cowling, Jane Crowden, Andrew King, Jeanette Mumford

Writing team for *Numbers and the number system 3*
Mark Adams, Lynn Huggins–Cooper, Jeanette Mumford, Andrew King, Marion Reynolds

The writers and publishers would like to thank the many schools and individuals
who trialled lessons for Cambridge Mathematics Direct.

NOTICE TO TEACHERS
It is illegal to reproduce any part of this work in material form (including photocopying and electronic storage)
except under the following circumstances:
(i) where you are abiding by a licence granted to your school or institution by the Copyright Licensing Agency;
(ii) where no such licence exists, or where you wish to exceed the terms of a licence, and you have
gained the written permission of Cambridge University Press;
(iii) where you are allowed to reproduce without permission under the provisions of Chapter 3 of
the Copyright, Designs and Patents Act 1988.

<u>Abbreviations and symbols</u>
IP   Interactive picture
CM   Copymaster
A   is practice work
B   develops ideas
C   is extension work
★   if needed, helps with work in A

Contents

Numbers (N): Counting, properties of numbers and number sequences

N1	**Counting in ones, tens and hundreds**	
N1.1	Counting collections	5
N1.2	Ones and tens beyond 100	7
N1.3	Ones, tens and hundreds	8
N2	**Twos**	
N2.1	Odds and evens	9
N2.2	Adding and subtracting odds and evens	11
N2.3	What if?	12
N3	**Steps and multiples**	
N3.1	Steps of 2, 3, 4 and 5	13
N3.3	Multiples of 2, 5 and 10	14
N3.4	Multiples of 50 and 100	15
N4	**Reasoning about numbers**	
N4.2	Puzzles and problems	16
N4.3	Grids	17
N4.4	Repeating patterns	18
N4.5	Extending patterns	19

Place value (PV): Place value and ordering

PV1	**Understanding place value**	
PV1.1	Introducing hundreds	21
PV1.2	Changing hundreds	23
PV1.3	Comparing numbers	24
PV2	**Exploring place value**	
PV2.1	Investigating 3-digit numbers	26
PV2.2	Adding and subtracting 1, 10 or 100	29
PV2.3	Numbers between	31
PV3	**Using place value**	
PV3.1	Ordering whole numbers	32
PV3.2	Comparing	34

PV3.3	Reading Scales	36

Rounding (R): Estimating and rounding

R1	**Estimating and rounding**	
R1.2	Number lines	38
R1.3	Rounding to 10 and 100	40

Fractions (F): Fractions

F1	**Simple fractions**	
F1.1	Fractions of shapes	42
F1.2	Equal and unequal	43
F1.3	Fractions of a set	44
F1.4	Further fractions of a set	46
F1.5	Simple fraction patterns	48
F2	**Extending fractions**	
F2.1	Thirds	49
F2.2	Halves and quarters	51
F2.3	Tenths	53
F2.4	Fractions of shapes	55
F2.5	More fractions of sets	56
F3	**Comparing fractions**	
F3.1	0–1 number line	57
F3.2	Number line to 10 (quarters)	58
F3.3	Tenths on a number line	59
F3.4	Estimating fractions	61
F3.5	Fraction patterns	62

N1.1 Counting collections

Key idea | We can make counting easier by grouping. One way of counting using grouping is keeping a tally.

B1 Steven jumped for 1 minute.
Tanya kept a tally of the number of jumps.

a What did Tanya do to help her count?

b How many jumps did she count?

B2 Hassan also counted Steven's jumps.

a How many jumps did he count?

b What makes Hassan's chart different from Tanya's?

B3 Kylie did 74 jumps.

  a Draw Tanya's tally.

  b Draw Hassan's tally.

C1 **a** Draw this tally chart.

	1	2	3	4	5	6
Tally						
Total						

Throw a dice.

Keep a tally of how many times you score each number.

Stop when you have scored any number 6 times.

  b Which number did you score 6 times?

  c Which number did you score least often?

Key idea We can make counting easier by grouping. One way of counting using grouping is keeping a tally.

N1.2 Ones and tens beyond one hundred

Key idea: We can count in ones and tens on and back from any 2–digit or 3–digit number.

B1
a. Count on six from 53.
b. Count on five from 121.
c. Count on eight from 256.

B2
a. Count back seven from 79.
b. Count back four from 284.
c. Count back three from 561.

B3
a. Count on fifty from 30.
b. Count on thirty from 145.
c. Count on eighty from 370.

B4 Draw this number track in your book.

				462	463	464		

a. Where would 458 be? Write it in.
b. Where would 466 be? Write it in.
c. Draw your own number track. Make up 2 questions about it.

N1 Counting in 1s, 10s and 100s

N1.3 Ones, tens and hundreds

Key idea | We can count on and back in ones, tens and hundreds from any 2–digit or 3–digit number.

B1 Describe these sequences. Write the next 2 numbers in each one.

a 53, 63, 73, . . .

b 137, 127, 117, . . .

c 645, 545, 445, . . .

d 219, 319, 419, . . .

B2 Copy these sequences and fill in the missing numbers.

a 16, ☐, 56, 76, 96, 116, ☐, 156

b ☐, 125, 135, ☐, 155, 165, ☐, 185

c 53, ☐, 453, 653, ☐

B3 Make up 3 sequences. Write about them.

Choose a starting number. Make up a rule.

N1 Counting in 1s, 10s and 100s

N 2.1 Odds and evens

> **Key idea**
> A number that has 0, 2, 4, 6 or 8 as its units digit is even.
> A number that has 1, 3, 5, 7 or 9 as its units digit is odd.

A1 The labels show how many pegs are in each bag.
Write each number and whether it is odd or even.

	odd or even?
47	
32	
90	
54	
65	
79	

A2 Write down the even numbers between

a 44 and 54   b 27 and 37

A3 Write down the odd numbers between

a 32 and 42   b 68 and 78

N2 Twos

B1 Write down the odd numbers

  a before 75, 63, 91

  a after 89, 71, 99

B2 Write down the even numbers

  a before 50, 72, 66

  b after 56, 68, 98

B3 Write the next 3 numbers in these sequences.

  a 47, 49, 51, 53, ☐, ☐, ☐

  b 78, 76, 74, 72, ☐, ☐, ☐

  c 63, 65, 67, ☐, ☐, ☐

  d 25, 23, 21, ☐, ☐, ☐

Key idea | A number that has 0, 2, 4, 6 or 8 as its units digit is even. A number that has 1, 3, 5, 7 or 9 as its units digit is odd.

N2.2 Adding and subtracting odds and evens

Key idea | If you add two even numbers the answer is even.
If you add two odd numbers the answer is also even.

There is an even number of socks in each laundry basket.

a 12
b 6
c 4
d 8
e 20

A1 Add together the numbers on 2 baskets to make different totals.

For example 8 + 6 = 14

Make as many different totals as you can.

A2 Take 1 sock out of each basket.
Write down the new number of socks in each one.

a 12 − 1 = 11

A3 Make subtraction sentences about taking an odd number of socks from each of the baskets.

For example a 11 − 5 = 6

A4 Complete this sentence.

When I subtract an odd number from an odd number . . .

B1 You need number cards 1 – 9.

Put your cards in a square so that the difference between each pair of joined cards is odd.

Can you find another way?

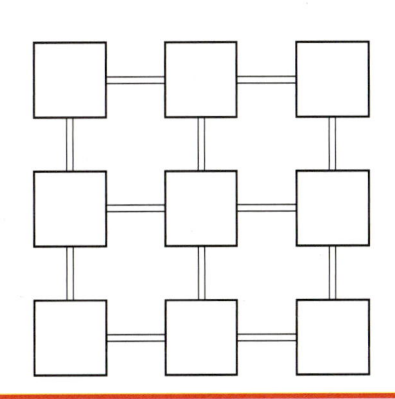

N2 Twos

11

N 2.3 What if?

| Key idea | When we ask ourselves 'what if?' we make up interesting questions to answer. |

A1 You have three 1–6 dice.
What <u>even</u> totals can you make?

$1 + 1 + 4 = 6$

List the numbers from 4 to 18 like this.

Total		Dice score
4 =		1 + 1 + 2
6 =		☐ + ☐ + ☐
8 =		☐ + ☐ + ☐

B1 The 1-digit odd numbers are 1, 3, 5, 7 and 9.

Use 4 of these odd numbers to make even numbers up to 20.

What numbers can you make?

You can use an odd number more than once.

$1 + 3 + 1 + 3 = 8$

B2 This time you can only use these odd numbers.

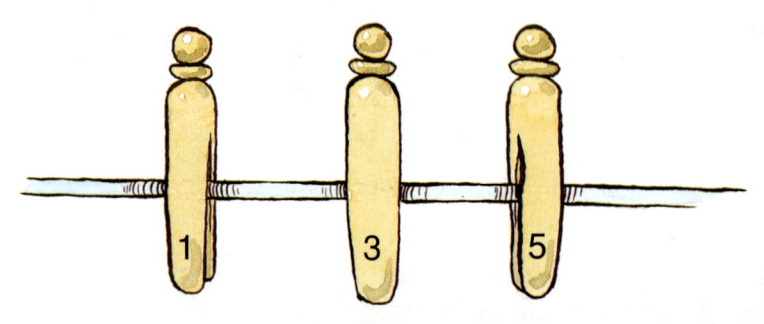

Which even numbers can you make?

N3.1 Steps of 2, 3, 4 and 5

> **Key idea** We can count on and back in steps of 2, 3, 4, 5, 10 or 100 from any small number.

B1 Find the missing numbers.
Write the sequence like this. **a** 18, 20, 22, 24, 26, 28

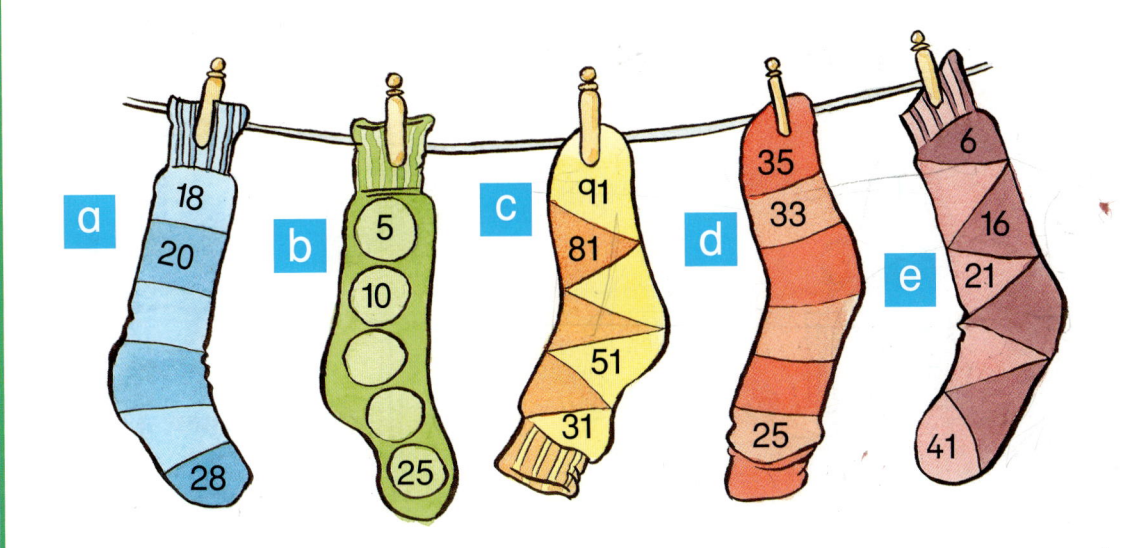

a: 18, 20, ..., ..., ..., 28
b: 5, 10, ..., ..., 25
c: 91, ..., 81, ..., ..., 51, ..., 31
d: 35, 33, ..., ..., ..., 25
e: 6, ..., ..., 16, ..., 21, ..., ..., ..., 41

B2 Find the missing numbers in these sequences.

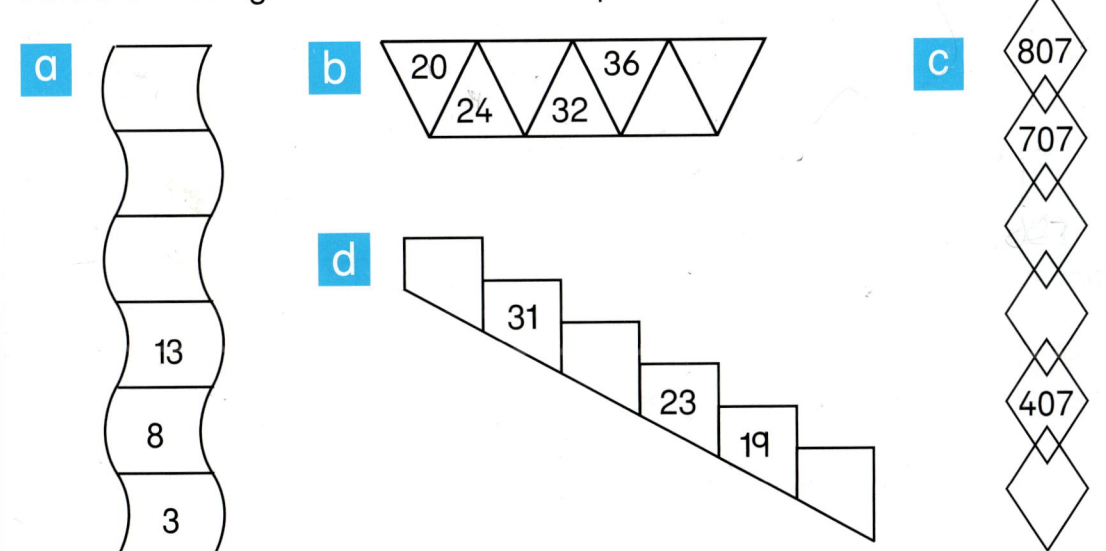

a: ..., ..., 13, ..., 8, ..., 3

b: 20, ..., 24, ..., ..., 32, ..., 36

c: 807, ..., 707, ..., ..., ..., ..., 407

d: ..., 31, ..., ..., 23, ..., 19, ...

B3 What will the next 3 numbers be in each sequence in B1 and B2?

C1 Make up 2 sequences of your own to or from 100.
What do you notice about the units digits?

N3 Steps and multiples

N3.3 Multiples of 2, 5 and 10

> **Key idea** We can tell if a 2- or 3-digit number is a multiple of 2, 5, or 10 by looking at the last digit.

This is a number sifter machine.

The machine contains the numbers: 6, 45, 90, 60, 95, 18, 54, 15, 25, 30, 20, 52, 10, 36, 55, 35, 70, 26. It sorts them into Box A (Multiples of 2), Box B (Multiples of 5), and Box C (Multiples of 10).

A1 Write down which numbers will fall into

 a. Box A
 b. Box B
 c. Box C

A2 Write the numbers which are

 a. multiples of 5 (175, 160, 151, 153, 195, 105)
 b. multiples of 2 (122, 127, 164, 178, 106, 152)
 c. multiples of 10 (190, 170, 106, 130, 102, 200)

B1
 a. Write the multiple of 10 before 180.
 b. Write the multiple of 5 after 185.
 c. Write the next multiple of 2 after 128.

B2 Draw a machine that only has multiples of 2 in it.

N3.4 Multiples of 50 and 100

| Key idea | We can count in steps of 50 and 100. |

A1 Find the missing numbers in these number lines.

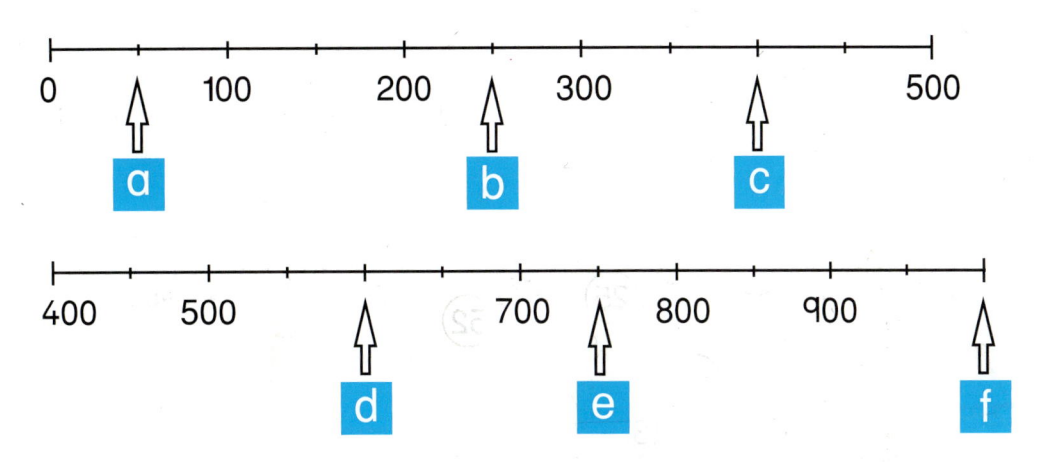

0 — a — 100 — 200 — b — 300 — c — 500

400 — 500 — d — 700 — e — 800 — 900 — f

A2 Write 3 different multiples of 50 between 300 and 700.

B1 Find the missing numbers.

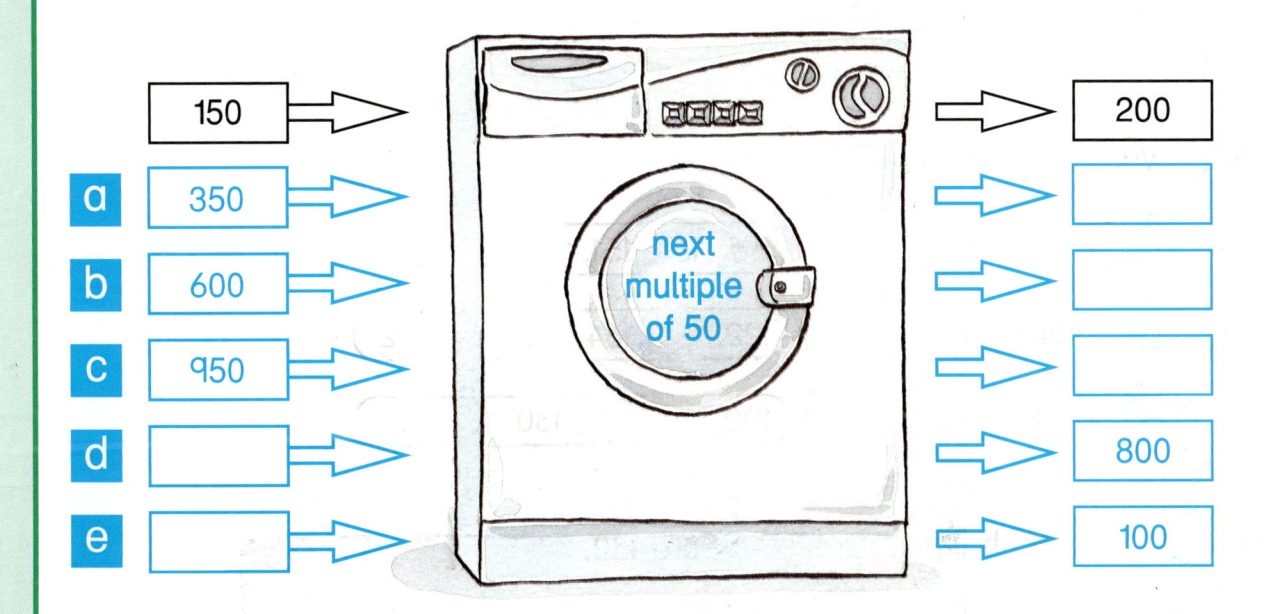

150 → → 200

a 350 → →
b 600 → →
c 950 → →
d ___ → → 800
e ___ → → 100

(next multiple of 50)

B2 Write down 3 things you know about multiples of 50 and 100.

C1 The washing machine is now going back 50.
What do the numbers become this time?

N3 Steps and Multiples

15

N4.2 Puzzles and problems

Key idea | We can solve a problem and then change it by asking 'What if...?'

B1 Choose 4 different numbers.

Find as many different equations as you can.

4   9
1
7   10
5   6

B2 What if 2 of the numbers are the same?

How many different equations can you make now?

C1 Choose 5 different numbers.

Find as many different equations as you can.

C2 Ask your own 'What if?...' question.

N4.3 Grids

> **Key idea** Sometimes, seeing a pattern helps us solve problems or puzzles.

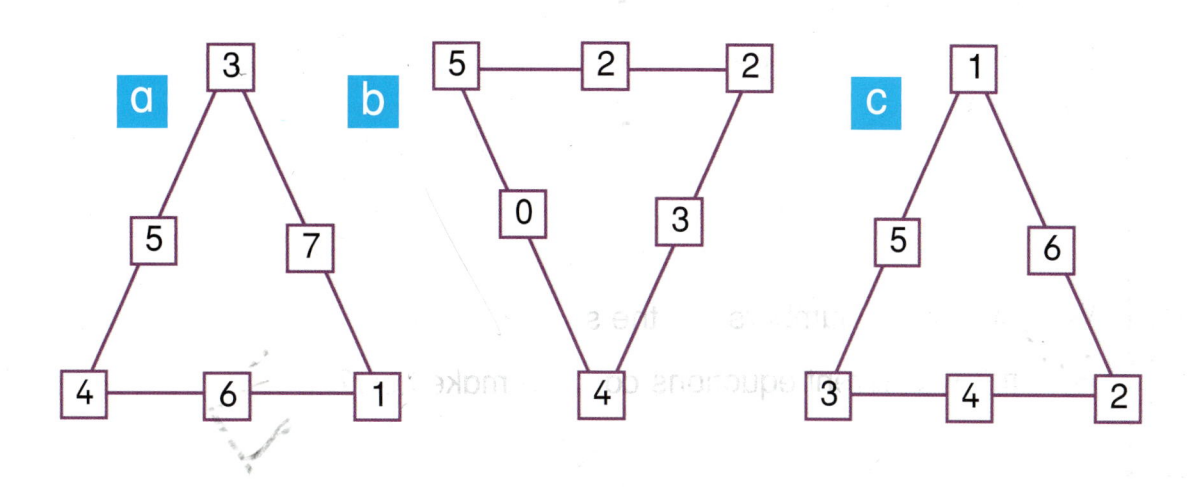

★1

a) Triangle with vertices 3, 4, 1 and sides 5, 7, and 4—6—1.
b) Triangle with top 5—2—2, sides 0, 3, and bottom 4.
c) Triangle with vertex 1, sides 5, 6, and bottom 3—4—2.

Add up the numbers on each side of the triangle.

Which triangle has sides that all add up to 9?

A1 Use cards 1–6.

Make a triangle with sides that total 9.

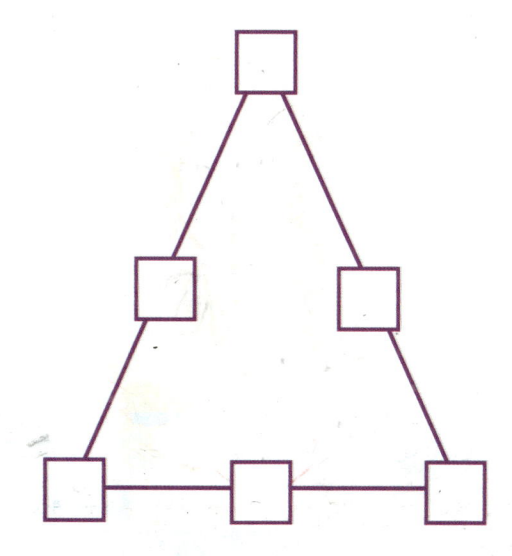

C1 Choose 6 consecutive numbers.
Make a triangle where the sum of the numbers on each side is the same.

N4 Reasoning about numbers

N4.4 Repeating patterns

Key idea | Being able to spot number patterns and talk about them can help you solve lots of number problems.

A1 Describe the pattern in each array to your partner. Write this down.

a

1	2	3	4	5
6	7	8	9	10

b

5	10	15
20	25	30
35	40	45
50	55	60

c

18	15	12	9	6	3
17	14	11	8	5	2
16	13	10	7	4	1

A2 Play 'What's that number?' on each one.

You need counters.

B1 Make up your own patterns on the CM 12.

18   N4 Reasoning about numbers

N4.5 Extending patterns

> **Key idea** If you can see patterns in numbers you can sometimes win games.

A1

a

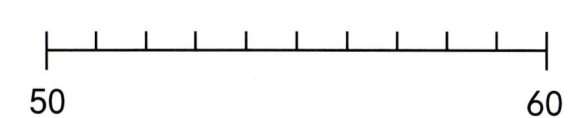

50 ———————————— 60

There are 5 odd numbers between 50 and 60.

Which numbers are they?

b

76 ———————————— 86

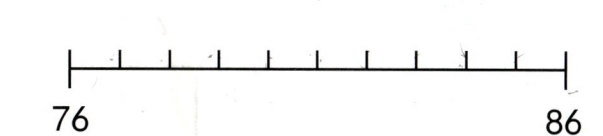

There are 4 even numbers between 76 and 86.

Which numbers are they?

B1

a

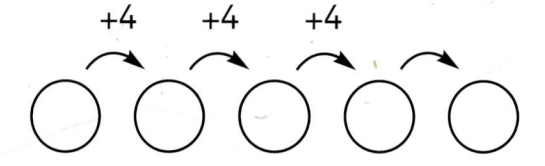

○ +4 → ○ +4 → ○ +4 → ○ → ○

Begin on any even number.
Jump on in 4s.
The numbers you land on are even.

Find 2 sequences that match the statement.

b

53 ———————————— 83

Jump in 5s from 53.
The units digits of all the numbers you land on are 3 or 8.

Find these numbers.

N4 Reasoning about numbers

B2 **a**

| 60 | | 100 |

Begin at 60.
Count on in steps of 2, 3, 4, 5 and 10.

Which steps land exactly on 100?

b Test these statements.
Show your working out.

Choose any 2-digit number.	47
Add 10.	47 + 10
There are 5 jumps of 2 between the 2 numbers.	47 → 57

Choose any 2-digit number.	47
Add 20.	47 + 20
There are 5 jumps of 4 between the 2 numbers.	47 → 67

C1 Play 'Jumping frogs' backwards!
The starting numbers are between 30 and 36.
Win a counter if you land exactly on zero.

You need CM13, a large counter for the frog, 12 counters and a dice marked 2, 2, 3, 4, 5, 10.

Key idea If you can see patterns in numbers you can sometimes win games.

PV1.1 Introducing hundreds

> **Key idea** | The position of a digit tells us its value.

B1 Write these numbers in words.

a 74   b 107   c 265   d 383   e 450

B2

a 423   b 342   c 234

a The digit 4 represents ☐ hundreds.

b The digit 4 represents

c The digit 4 represents

B3 Split the numbers into hundreds, tens and units.

a 275 = ☐ + 70 + 5

b 492 = 400 + ☐ + 2

c 316 = 300 + ☐ + ☐

d 108 = ☐ + ☐ + ☐

PV1 Understanding place value

B4 Look at IP 4.

Find and write down a number that is

a more than 300

b odd and more than 400

c a multiple of 10

d less than 200 and more than 80

Make up some puzzles like this.

Work with a partner.

Take turns to solve your partner's puzzle.

C1 Look back at B2.

Make each number 100 more.

Write what each digit represents.

Key idea | The position of a digit tells us its value.

1.2 Changing hundreds

> **Key idea** When we count on or back in 100s, the numbers in the tens and units position's stay the same.

You need 10 counters or cubes and CM 17.

Place all 10 counters in the sections of the board to make different numbers.

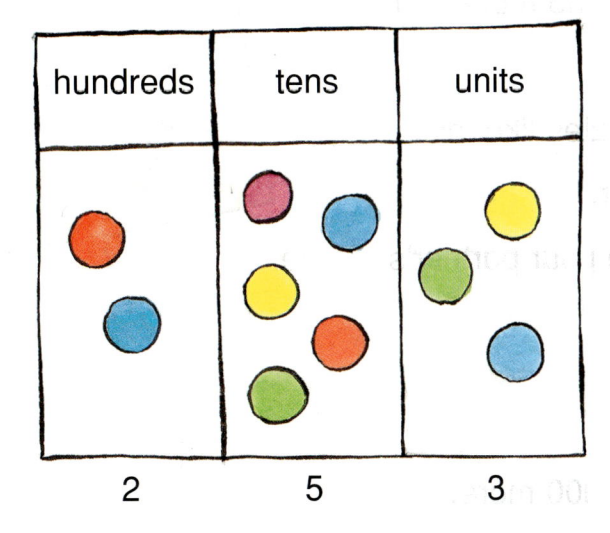

hundreds	tens	units
2	5	3

C1 What numbers between 200 and 300 can you make with 10 counters?

Write your numbers in a table like this:

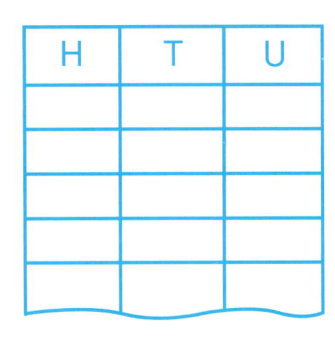

H	T	U

C2 What if ... the numbers are between _____ and _____?

Make a table to record your numbers.

C3 What if ... you had 20 cubes or counters?

PV1 Understanding place value

PV1.3 Comparing numbers

> **Key idea** We can put things in order and describe their position with special words.

Vest numbers: 85, 275, 382, 416, 139, 46, 201, 133

A1 Write these vest numbers in order. Start with the smallest number.

A2 What could the missing numbers on these vests be?

130 ☐ 133 ☐ ☐ ☐ 139

24 PV1 Understanding place value

B1 The cricket and tennis balls in this box are in a pattern.

Use the pattern to answer these questions.

You could use red and yellow counters to help.

- **a** Which ball is in the 12th position?
- **b** Is the 16th ball a cricket or a tennis ball?
- **c** Write the numbers of all the tennis balls.
- **d** What if the box held 30 balls?

  Name the balls in the 27th and 29th positions.

C1 Work with a partner.

Balls are arranged in a 100 square in the same pattern as in B1.

Where will the tennis balls be?

Key idea We can put things in order and describe their position with special words.

PV1 Understanding place value

PV2.1 Investigating 3-digit numbers

> **Key idea** The value of a digit depends on its position.

These runners have the same 3 digits on their vests.

"I've the largest 3-digit number..." — 532

"... and I've the smallest." — 235

A1 Copy the table.

Make 3-digit vest numbers for the orange and green teams

	digits	orange team largest 3-digit number	green team smallest 3-digit number
a	3 2 5	532	235
b	9 8 4		
c	6 1 7		
d	8 3 5		
e	7 9 9		

A2 Write what each digit represents in each pair of numbers in **a** to **e**

B1 Two runners have lost their ⬚0⬚ cards.

Which two 3-digit numbers might they have?

a ⬚4⬚ ⬚7⬚

b ⬚6⬚ ⬚3⬚

B2 **a** Sort the vests into their laundry bags.

506   640   505
650   560   606

0 tens   0 units

b Now order the numbers in each laundry bag from smallest to largest.

650   506   640
606   505   560

PV2 Exploring place value

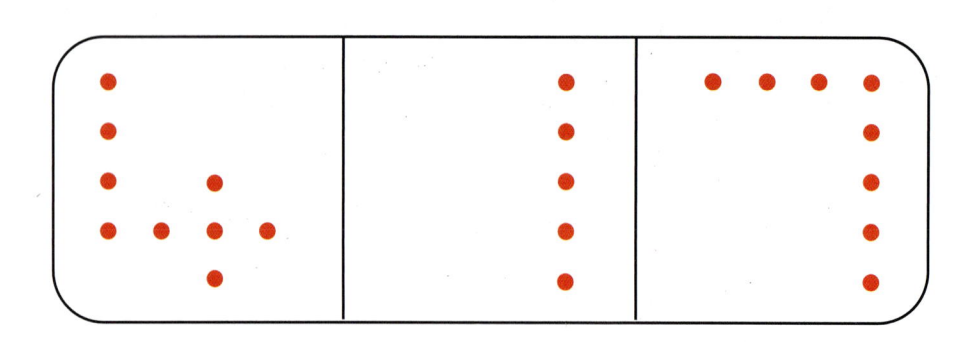

C1 Some of the lights on the electronics results board are out.

The board will only show the numbers 7, 4 and 1.

List the 3-digit numbers it can show where each digit is different.

C2 Look at your answers to C1.

Complete these sentences.

The largest number is _____

The smallest number is _____

The number nearest 500 is _____

The odd numbers are _____

C3 What if the board can show ⋮ more than once?

List this set of 3-digit numbers.

Begin with 1 in the hundreds place.

Key idea The value of a digit depends on its position.

PV2 Exploring place value

V2.2 Adding and subtracting 1, 10 or 100

> **Key idea** If you add or subtract 10 or 100, the units digit stays the same.

B1 Continue these sequences.

a 260, 270, 280, ☐, ☐, ☐

b 904, 903, 902, ☐, ☐, ☐

c 430, 530, 630, ☐, ☐, ☐

B2 Find the missing numbers a to e in this grid.

+	—— +1 —— →			
↓ +10	146	147	148	a
	156	c		
	b			
			d	e

B3 a Copy this table.

Work out the missing numbers.

Look for a pattern in your answers.

number	− 1 →	− 10 →	− 100 →
390	389	379	279
391			
401			
411			

b Write about any patterns you notice.

PV2 Exploring place value

C1 Bill counted the entry fee money.

He wrote £9.40 on the bag.

He asked some people to check.

Ali counted 1p more and wrote down £9.41

Use the diagram to work out the amount each checker wrote down.

a £9.41 ← +1p   −1p → ☐ b

c ☐ ← +10p   −10p → ☐ d

£9.40

e ☐ ← +100p   −100p → ☐ f

C2 Look at your answers to C1.

What is the difference between the greatest and the least amounts?

Check your answer. Use a different way to calculate it.

Key idea If you add or subtract 10 or 100, the units digit stays the same.

30   PV2 Exploring place value

PV2.3 Numbers between

Key idea: We can compare two numbers and find a number between them.

★ 1 Which is more?
- a) 506 g or 560 g
- b) £7.50 or £8.50

Which is longer?
- c) 175 m or 157 m
- d) 216 km or 126 km

Which is lighter?
- e) 7.3 kg or 5.3 kg
- f) 10.4 kg or 14.0 kg

Which is less?
- g) 630p or 713p
- h) 998 m or 989 m

B1

a) Imran lifted between 16 kg and 20 kg. What weight in kilograms might he have lifted?

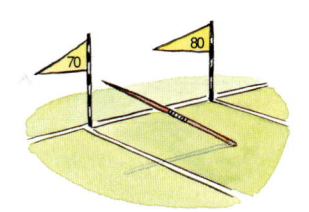

b) Kenny's javelin landed between the 70 m and 80 m marks. What distance might he have thrown?

c) Gina's prize cost between £8 and £9. What might it have cost?

d) Jenny has run between 80 m and 120 m. How far in metres might she have run?

B2

"I won. I lifted 14 kg."

"I lifted 13 kg."

What weight might the second-placed athlete have lifted?

PV2 Exploring place value

31

PV3.1 Ordering whole numbers

Key idea | When we order 3-digit numbers we look first at the hundreds digit, then at the tens digit and finally at the units digit.

A1

Match the bottles to the labels.
Write in figures how much liquid is in each bottle.

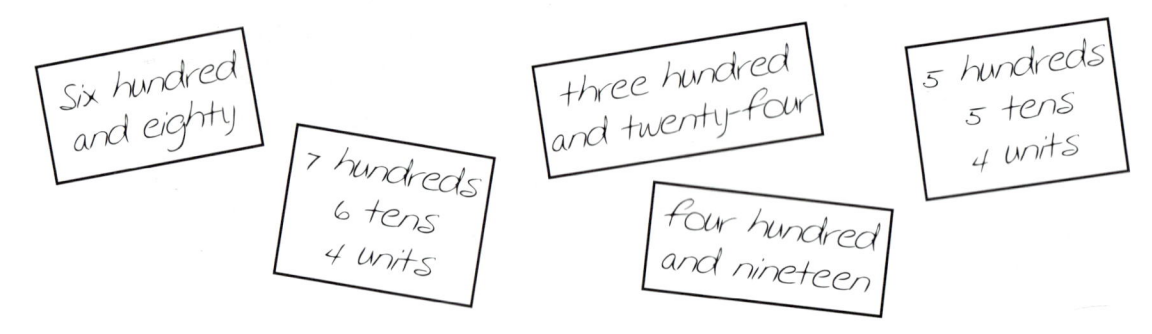

- Six hundred and eighty
- 7 hundreds 6 tens 4 units
- three hundred and twenty-four
- four hundred and nineteen
- 5 hundreds 5 tens 4 units

A2 List these containers in order. Begin with the smallest number.

406   416   401   410   461

A3
- a) 100 + 30 + 7 =
- b) 500 + 80 + 6 =
- c) 600 + 90 + 0 =
- d) 900 + 0 + 3 =

700   9
40
749

32   PV3 Using place value

B1 Find the missing numbers

a 365 = 300 + ⬚ + 5

b 217 = 200 + 10 + ⬚

c 535 = ⬚ + 30 + 5

d 877 = 800 + ⬚ + ⬚

B2 Secret recipes

How much liquid will the mad professor put in each flask?

- Solve the clues.
- Work out the number.

Recipe 1 (shows _ 6 _)

Secret recipe 1
- more than 250
- even number
- has a 6 in the tens column
- the sum of the 3 digits is 9.

Secret recipe 2
- less than 400
- odd number
- has a five in the tens column
- the sum of the digits is 8

Recipe 2

Secret recipe 3
- more than 500 and less than 800
- the hundreds digit is an even number
- tens and units digits are the same
- the sum of the 3 digits is 12

C1 Invent a secret recipe for your friend to solve.

Key idea When we order 3-digit numbers we look first at the hundreds digit, then at the tens digit and finally at the units digit.

PV3 Using place value

PV3.2 Comparing

Key idea | A number lying between 2 numbers is greater than the first number and smaller than the second.

B1 The professor tested 6 rockets.

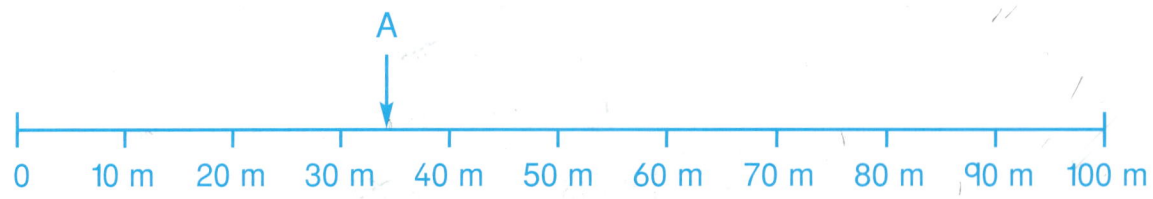

Copy the number line. Mark where each rocket fell. Rocket A is done for you.

rocket	distance flown
A	34 m
B	78 m
C	58 m
D	45 m
E	89 m
F	61 m

```
        A
        ↓
|---|---|---|---|---|---|---|---|---|---|
0  10m 20m 30m 40m 50m 60m 70m 80m 90m 100m
```

B2 Use the number line to answer these questions.

Which 2 rockets:

a. flew more than 70 m?

b. flew less than 50 m?

c. landed closest together?

Which rocket:

d. flew almost 90 m?

e. landed closest to 60 m?

f. landed half way between 40 m and 50 m?

g. flew 20 m further than rocket C?

PV3 Using place value

B3 Play 'Compare'.

You need a partner, number cards 1–9 and counters.

1. Shuffle the cards.
2. Spread them face down on the table.
3. Take 4 cards each.
4. Check that you have at least 1 odd and 1 even card. If not, do a swap.
5. Choose 3 of your 4 cards to make each target number.
6. Compare answers.

The player closest to the target wins a counter.

The winner is the player with the most counters.

3-digit target numbers

- highest number
- lowest number
- largest even number
- smallest even number
- largest odd number
- smallest odd number
- number furthest from 500
- number closest to 250
- number nearest to 750

> **Key idea** A number lying between 2 numbers is greater than the first number and smaller than the second.

PV3 Using place value

PV3.3 Reading scales

> **Key idea** | The marked divisions help us to read amounts on a scale.

B1 Write down the weight of each box.

a

b

c

d

B2 Read the pressure gauges.

a Write down the number that each gauge shows.

b Find the difference in pressure between the two gauges.

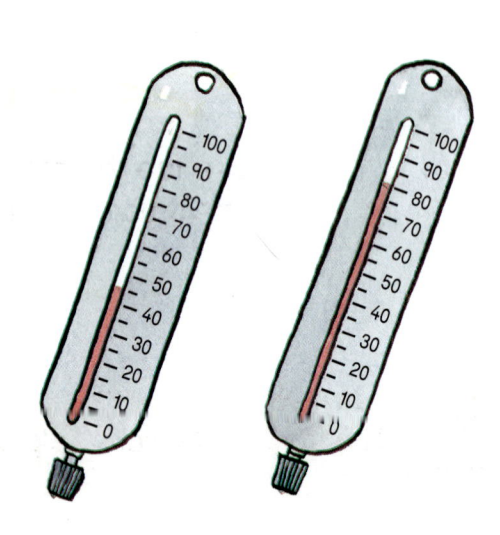

B3 Work out the drop in pressure that these gauges show.

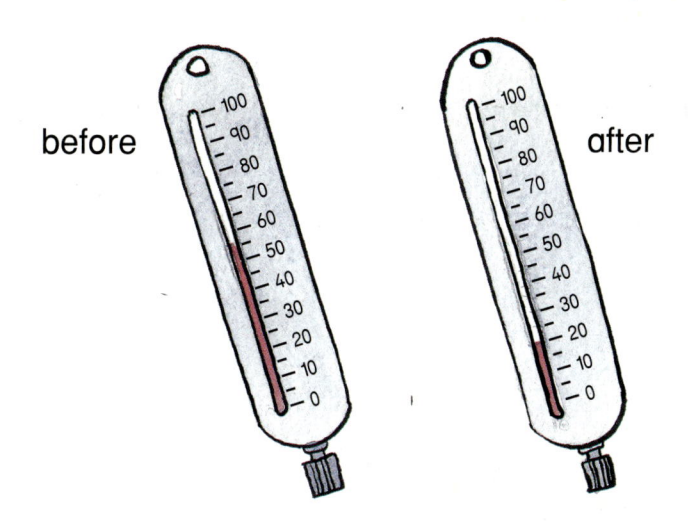

before   after

B4 This table shows the temperatures of the Mad Professor's experiments taken at 10 o'clock and how they changed.

Work out the temperatures taken at 10.30 am.

	temperature at 10.00 am	change	temperature at 10.30 am
Experiment A	17 °C	37 °C warmer	
Experiment B	45 °C	15 °C warmer	
Experiment C	62 °C	19 °C warmer	
Experiment D	34 °C	48 °C warmer	
Professor's tea	85 °C	77 °C cooler	

Use the thermometer to help you if you want.

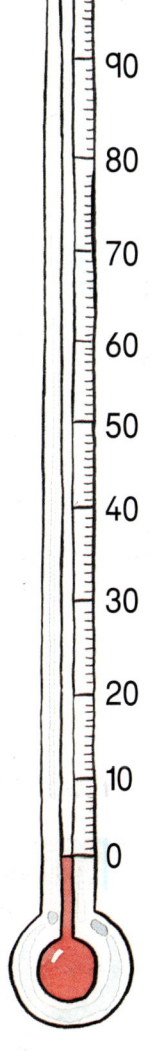

Key idea The marked divisions help us to read amounts on a scale.

PV3 Using place value

37

R1.2 Number lines

> **Key idea** We can estimate the position of numbers on a number line.

A1

Draw the washing lines in your book.
Put the numbers in the right order.

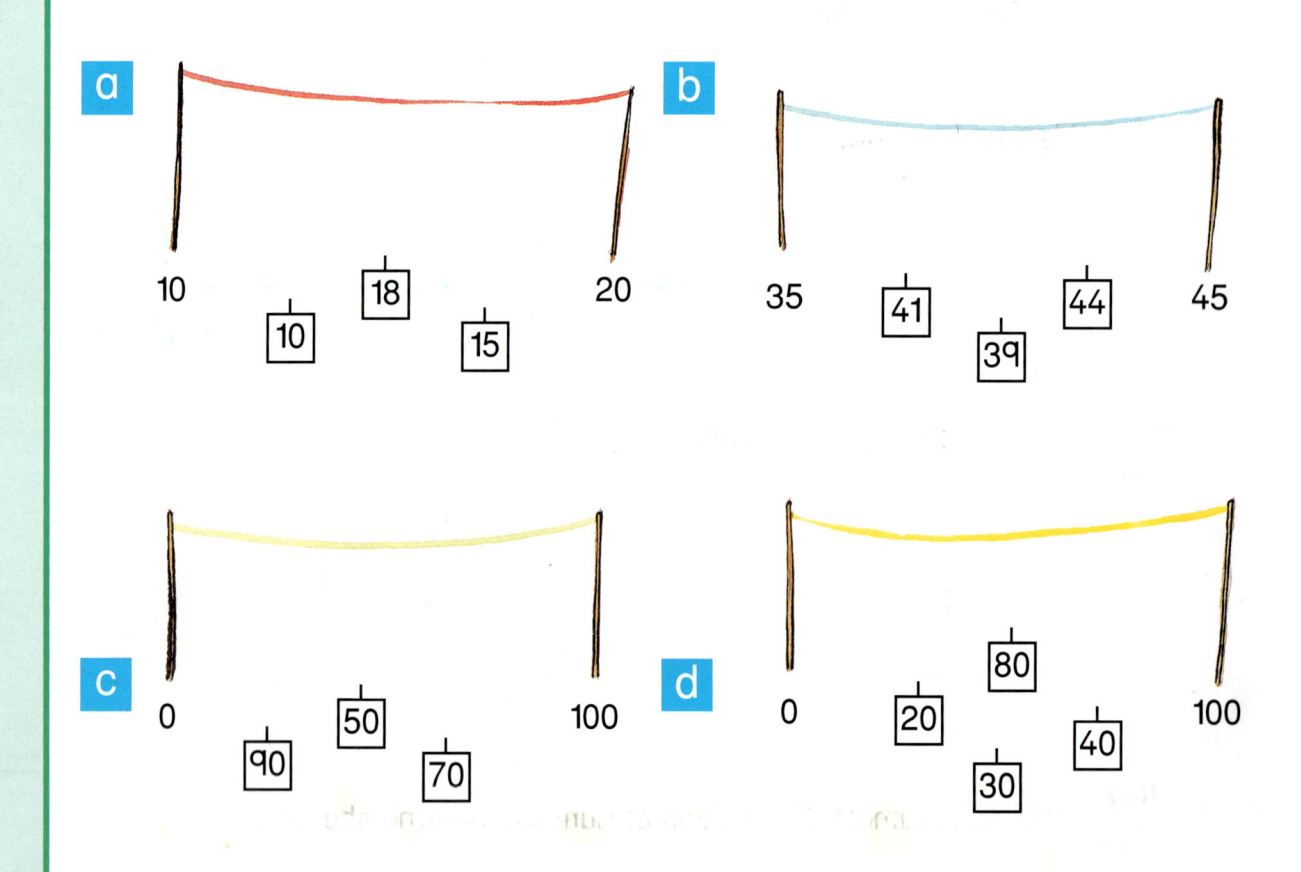

a 10 ... 20   numbers: 18, 10, 15

b 35 ... 45   numbers: 41, 44, 39

c 0 ... 100   numbers: 50, 90, 70

d 0 ... 100   numbers: 20, 80, 40, 30

38 R1 Estimating and rounding

B1 Draw the number lines. Mark the points.

a
```
|————|————|————|————|
0                    20
```

1, 5, 10, 16

b
```
|————|————|————|
30              60
```

40, 50, 55, 58

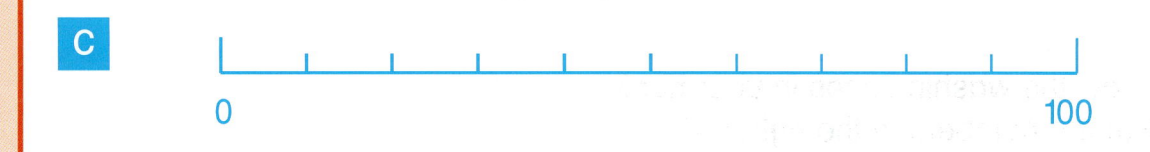

c
```
|——|——|——|——|——|——|——|——|——|——|
0                                100
```

15, 30, 65, 80

C1 Draw this number line.

```
|————————————————————————|
0                        100
```

Put these numbers on your line.

67   75   44
   12
24   93   38
   29 56   16

Key idea We can estimate the position of numbers on a number line.

R1 Estimating and rounding   39

R1.3 Rounding to 10 and 100

| Key idea | We can decide whether to round numbers up or down by looking at the units or tens digits. |

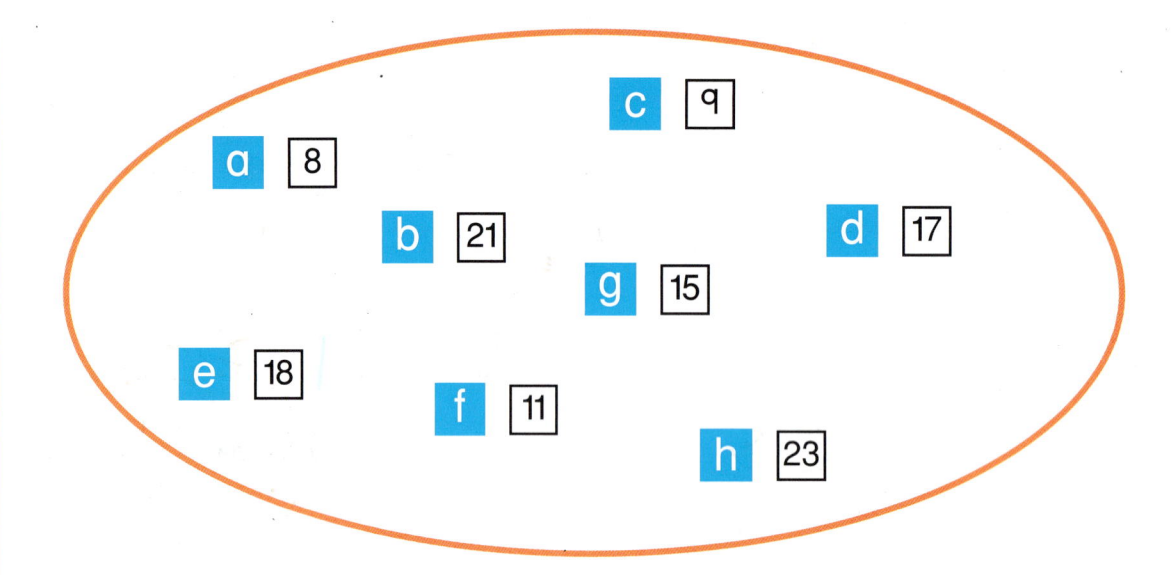

★1

Look at the numbers in the hoop.
Round each number to the nearest 10.

a 8
b 21
c 9
d 17
e 18
f 11
g 15
h 23

★2 Which number is the odd one out?

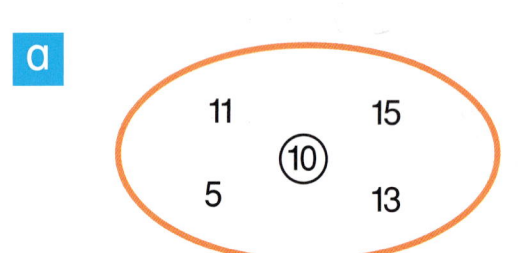

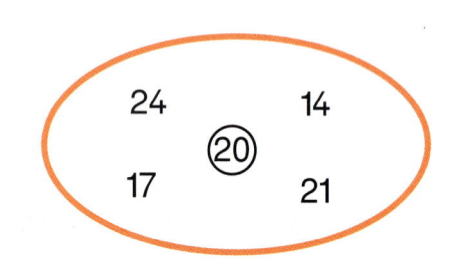

a
11 15
(10)
5   13

b
24   14
(20)
17   21

A1 Round the numbers on the baskets to the nearest 10.
Which is the odd one out?

a ?
72 65
79 71

b ?
11 14
18 7

c ?
54 42
48 53

d ?
36 48
41 44

R1 Estimating and rounding

A2 Change each 'odd one out' in A1 so it rounds to the same number as the other 3 numbers.

A3 Round the numbers on the flying saucers to the nearest 100.

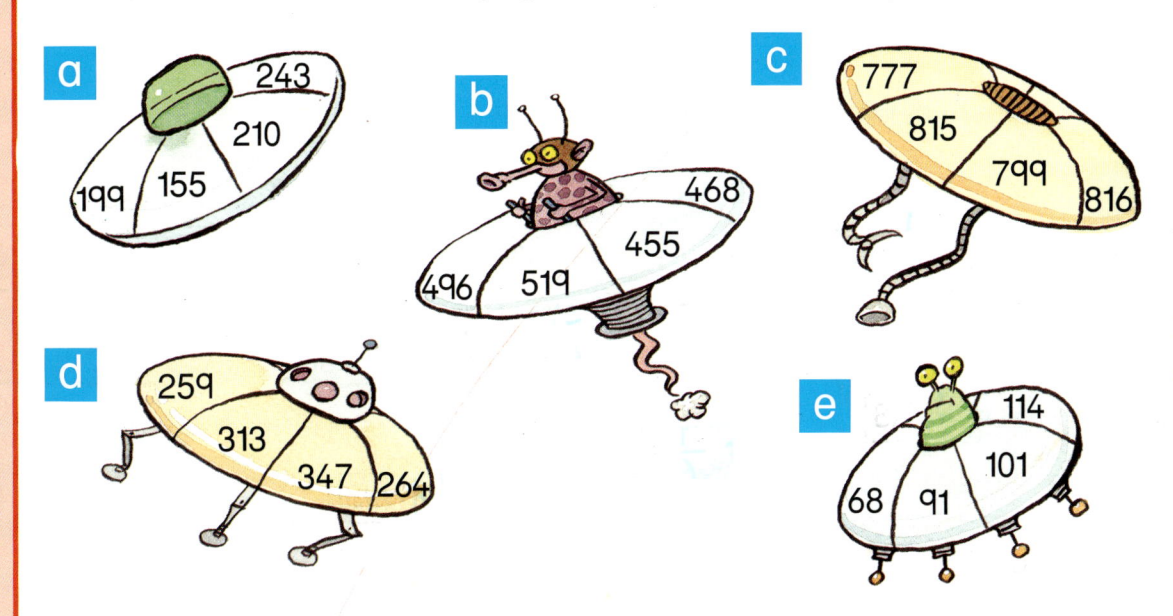

a) 243, 210, 199, 155

b) 468, 455, 496, 519

c) 777, 815, 799, 816

d) 259, 313, 347, 264

e) 114, 101, 68, 91

A4 Choose another number to go on each flying saucer.

B1 Find 9 numbers that round to 70.

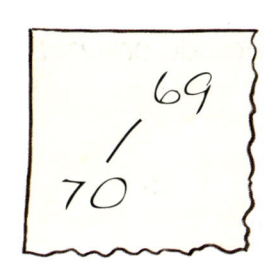

69
70

B2 Find 20 numbers that round to 300.

C1
a) Choose a tens number.
b) Write down all the numbers that round to it.
c) Repeat for another tens number.
d) Can you find a pattern?

Key idea We can decide whether to round numbers up or down by looking at the units or tens digit.

R1 Estimating and rounding

41

F1.1 Fractions of shapes

> **Key idea** The number at the bottom of a fraction shows how many equal parts the whole has been divided into.

A1 What fraction is each piece of the whole?

a b c

d e f

A2 How many equal pieces has each shape in A1 been cut into?

B1 You need CM 27.

Write each fraction in words.

B2 Six children share a whole cake.

What fraction do they each eat?

C1 Make up 5 fraction puzzles for your friend.

F1 Simple fractions

F1.2 Equal and unequal

> **Key idea** A part of the shape is only a fraction of the whole if the shape has been divided into equal parts.

A1 Which shapes show one quarter shaded?

a   b   c   d

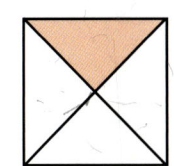

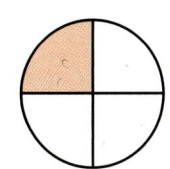

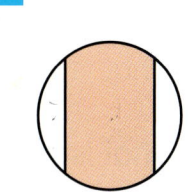

A2 Which shapes show one third shaded?

a   b   c   d

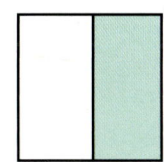

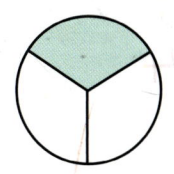

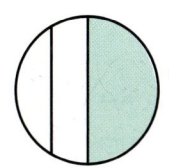

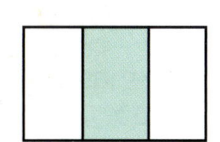

A3 Which shapes do not show one tenth shaded?

a   b   c   d

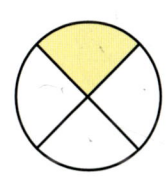

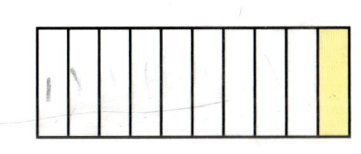

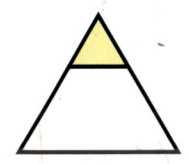

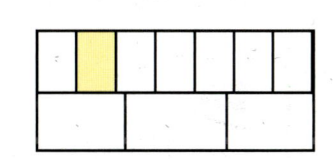

B1 Draw shapes and show these fractions on them.

a $\frac{1}{2}$ b $\frac{1}{3}$ c $\frac{1}{10}$ d $\frac{1}{4}$ e $\frac{1}{5}$

B2 Draw shapes and make them show

a 2 parts but not halves

b 3 parts but not thirds

F1 Simple fractions

F1.3 Fractions of a set

Key idea — We can find fractions of sets.

You need cubes.

★1 What is $\frac{1}{2}$ of 6?

★2 What is $\frac{1}{4}$ of 8?

★3 What is $\frac{1}{5}$ of 5?

A1 Find how many there are in

a $\frac{1}{4}$ of 20   b $\frac{1}{5}$ of 15   c $\frac{1}{10}$ of 10

A2 There are 24 people.

How many of them make

a $\frac{1}{2}$?

b $\frac{1}{3}$?

c $\frac{1}{4}$?

d $\frac{1}{6}$?

e $\frac{1}{12}$?

f $\frac{1}{24}$?

Remember to use cubes.

44   F1 Simple fractions

B1 There are 8 hats. What fraction of the set is ringed?

B2 What fraction of each set is ringed?

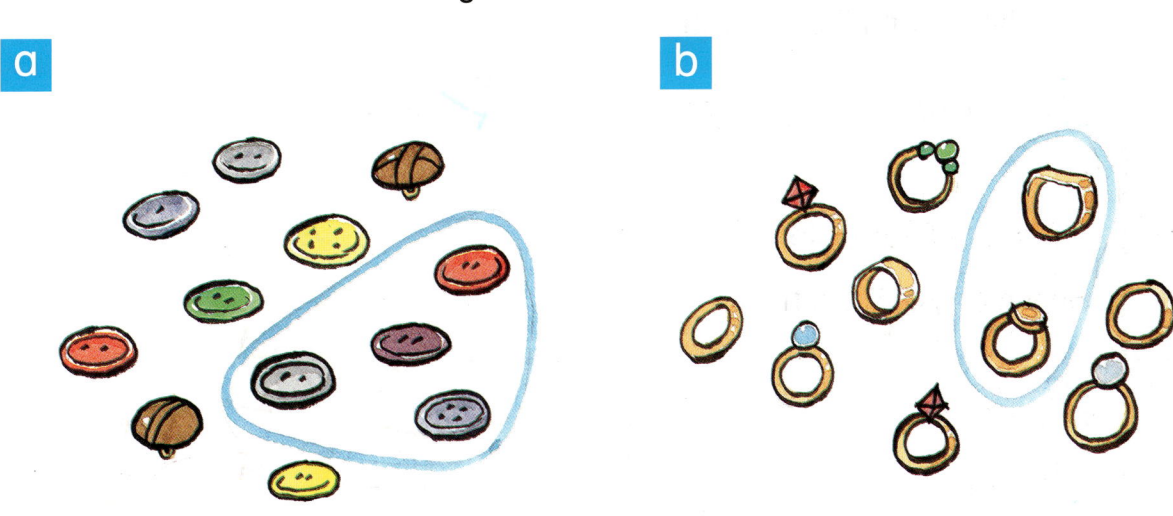

a

b

B3 Choose 4 even numbers less than 20. Find half of each.
You can use cubes to help you.

C1 Look at the people on IP 6. There are 30 of them.

One fifth are wearing hats.

Work out some other fraction facts about the people on the picture.

| Key idea | We can find fractions of sets. |

F1 Simple fractions

F1.4 Further fractions of a set

Key idea	We can find half of an odd number.

★1 Do A using paper shapes.

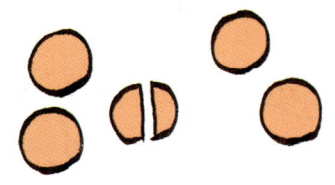

A1 Find half of all the numbers to 30.

You can use cubes.

B1 7 bananas are divided equally between 3 children.

How many does each child get?

B2 13 apples are divided equally between 4 children.

How many does each child get?

B3 21 rolls are divided equally between 5 children.

How many does each child get?

F1 Simple fractions

C1

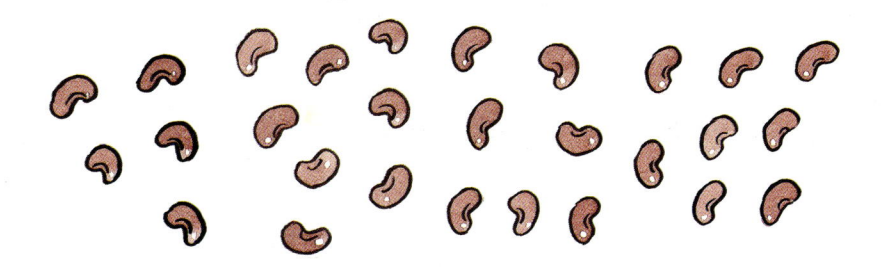

28 beans

1. Half of 28 is 14

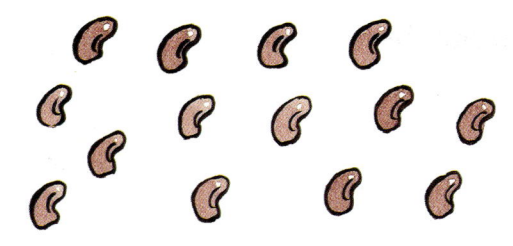

2. Half of 14 is 7

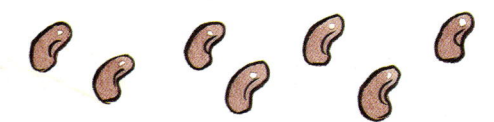

3. Half of 7 is $3\frac{1}{2}$

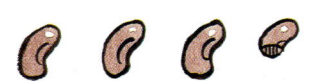

Do this for 30 beans.

Stop when you reach an answer that has $\frac{1}{2}$ in it.

C2 Repeat C1 for other numbers to 30.

Can you see a pattern?

Key idea We can find half of an odd number.

F1 Simple fractions

F1.5 Simple fraction problems

> **Key idea** We can solve problems involving fractions.

B1 You need cubes.

Make towers out of cubes that are

- **a** 8 cubes high; $\frac{1}{4}$ are white
- **b** 6 cubes high; $\frac{1}{3}$ are brown
- **c** 20 cubes high; $\frac{1}{5}$ are pink and $\frac{1}{4}$ are yellow

B2 Use cubes to make a 3 x 4 rectangle.
It must be $\frac{1}{6}$ green, $\frac{1}{3}$ blue and $\frac{1}{2}$ red.

C1 Complete the sentences.

- **a** There are 10 rabbits. $\frac{1}{2}$ are white.

    ☐ rabbits are white.

- **b** There are 18 cats. $\frac{1}{3}$ are ginger.

    6 cats are ginger.

- **c** I have 25 sweets. 5 are sherbet.

    5 of my sweets are sherbet.

- **d** $\frac{1}{2}$ the apples are green. 10 apples are green.

    I have 10 apples.

C2 Make up 2 fraction problems of your own.

48 F1 Simple fractions

F2.1 Thirds

> **Key idea** — We can find two thirds of shapes and sets.

★1 Look at each shape. Is it divided into thirds?

a   b 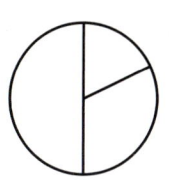   c

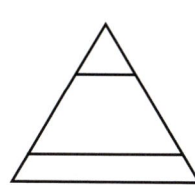

d 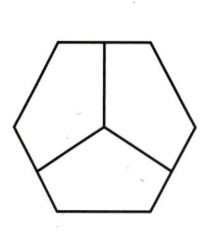   e    f

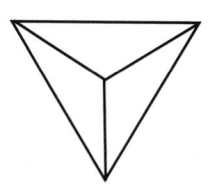

A1 Look at each sweet. Say whether $\frac{1}{3}$ or $\frac{2}{3}$ is shaded blue.

a   b    c

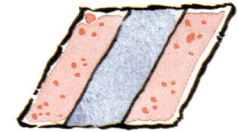

d    e

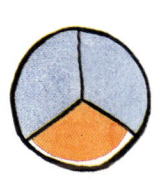

A2  12 sweets in a bag.

a How many in $\frac{1}{3}$ bag?

b How many in $\frac{2}{3}$ bag?

B1 You need CM 30.

F2 Extending fractions

C1 **a** How many cakes are chocolate squares?

b What fraction of the cakes is this?

C2 **a** How many cakes are not cherry cakes?

b What fraction of the cakes is this?

C3 **a** How many lollies are there?

b What fraction of the sweets is this?

C4 What fraction of the sweets are pink bars of chocolate?

C5 What fraction of the sweets are not chocolate?

C6 Two thirds of the cakes are sold. How many are left?

C7 Two thirds of the sweets are sold. How many are left?

Key idea	We can find two thirds of shapes and sets.

F2 extending fractions

F2.2 Halves and quarters

Key idea | Two quarters make one half.

A1 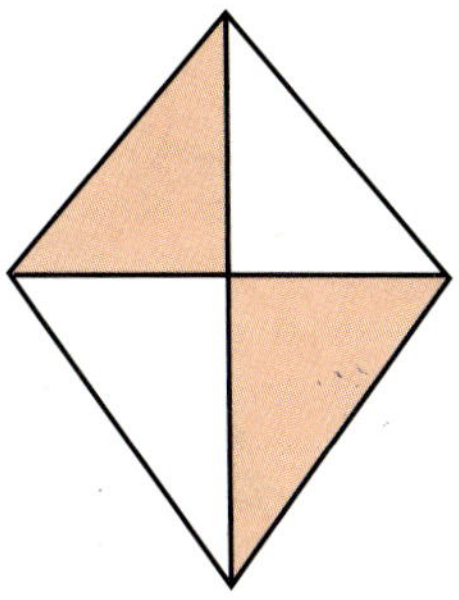
a How much is shaded?
b How much is not shaded?
c Is half shaded?

A2 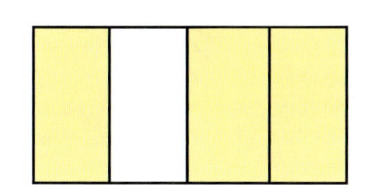
a How much is shaded?
b How much is not shaded?
c Is half shaded?

A3 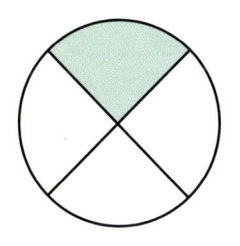
a How much is shaded?
b How much is not shaded?
c Is half shaded?

A4 Draw a square which is $\frac{1}{2}$ blue and $\frac{2}{4}$ red.

B1 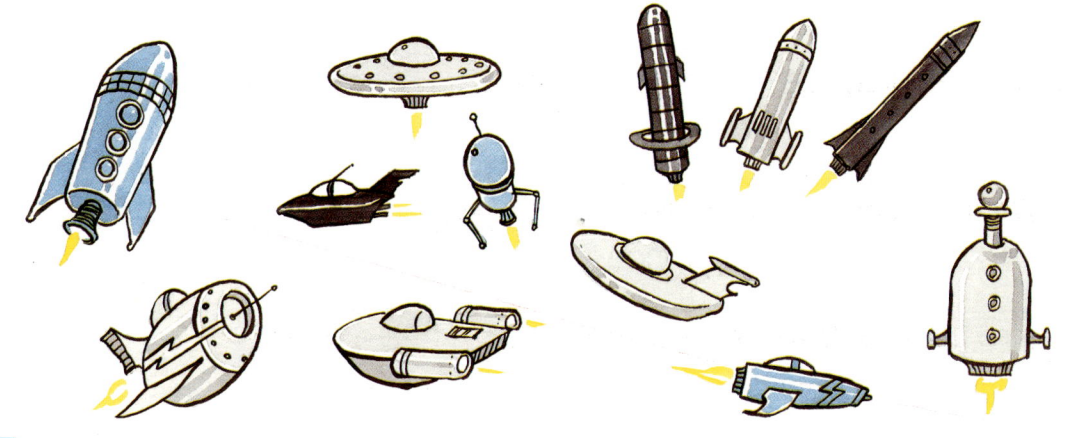
a What fraction of the spaceships are blue?
b What fraction of the spaceships are silver?
c What fraction of the spaceships are not silver?

F2 Extending fractions

51

B2

a $\frac{3}{4}$ of the aliens have itchy feet.

☐ have itchy feet.

b $\frac{1}{2}$ of the aliens have helmets at home. How many is that?

c $\frac{2}{4}$ of aliens wear a wig to parties. How many is that?

d Do more aliens wear wigs or helmets?

C Draw your own alien.

$\frac{3}{4}$ of its arms should be green.

$\frac{2}{4}$ of its eyes should be orange.

$\frac{1}{2}$ of its feet should be hairy.

| Key idea | Two quarters make one half. |

F2.3 Tenths

> **Key idea** Five tenths make one half.

A1 Some children have made some patterns:

Sharni   Robert    Claire

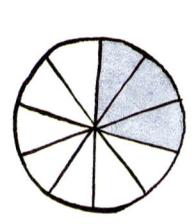

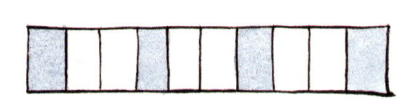

a Look at each pattern. What fraction has been shaded?

b Whose shape is half shaded?

c How many tenths has Robert coloured in?

A2 For each, say how many tenths are in the ring and how many outside.

a   b    c

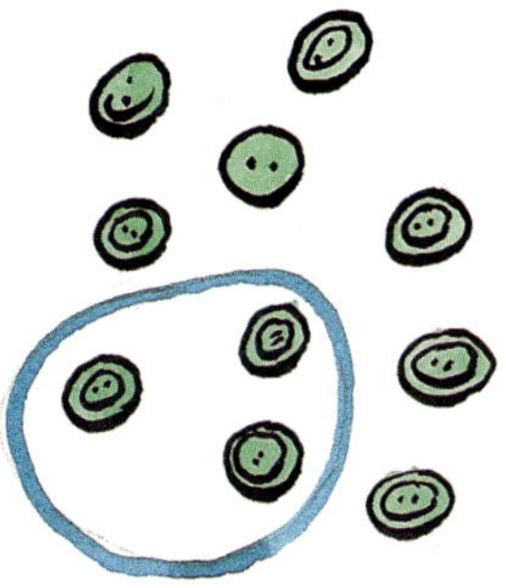

d 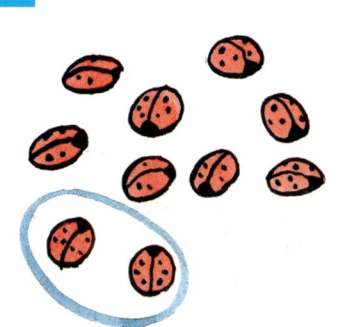   e    f

F2 Extending fractions   53

B1 **You need some cubes.**
Choose 3 colours.

Make a shape out of 20 cubes.

$\frac{1}{2}$ must be one colour.

$\frac{2}{10}$ must be your second colour.

$\frac{3}{10}$ must be your third colour.

C1 How many more tenths need to be coloured in so that $\frac{1}{2}$ of each shape is coloured in?

a

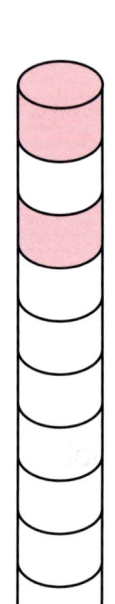

b

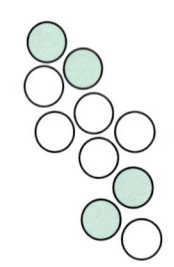

c

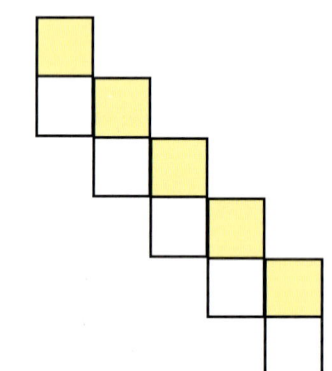

d

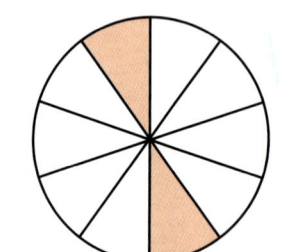

e

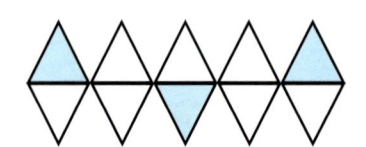

| Key idea | Five tenths make one half. |

54   F2 Extending fractions

F2.4 Fractions of shapes

Key idea | If we know what fraction of the whole we have, we can work out what the whole shape looks like.

A1 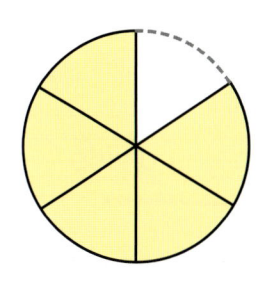
a How much is missing?
b Five sixths and ☐ make one whole.

A2 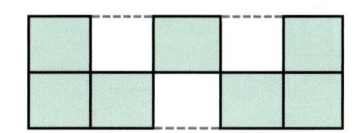
a How much is missing?
b Seven tenths and ☐ make one whole.

A3 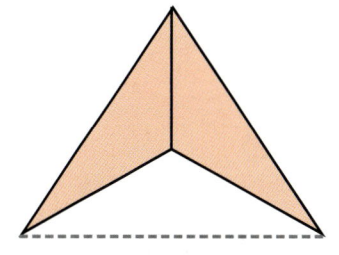
a How much is missing?
b ☐ and ☐ make one whole.

A4 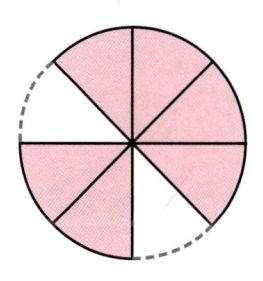
a How much is missing?
b ☐ and ☐ make one whole.

A5 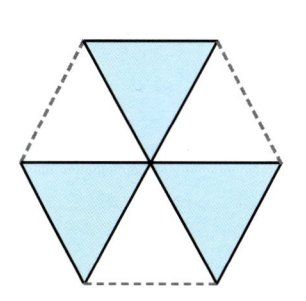
a How much is missing?
b ☐ and ☐ make one whole.
c Write your answer to b in a different way.

F2 Extending fractions

55

F2.5 More fractions of sets

> **Key idea** We can find $\frac{3}{4}$, $\frac{2}{5}$, $\frac{4}{10}$,... of sets of objects.

B1 You need cubes or counters.

Investigate the different fractions you can make when you divide

- **a** 15 into fifths
- **b** 12 into thirds
- **c** 14 into sevenths

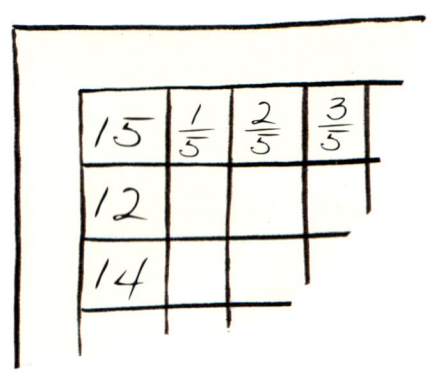

	$\frac{1}{5}$	$\frac{2}{5}$	$\frac{3}{5}$
15			
12			
14			

C1 Investigate the different fractions you can make when you divide

- **a** 30 into thirds
- **b** 30 into fifths
- **c** 30 into tenths
- **d** 30 into halves

C2 Which of the fractions are equivalent?

F2 Extending fractions

F3.1 0-1 number line

| Key idea | We can find $\frac{1}{4}$ by halving and then halving again. |

★1 **You need paper shapes, scissors and glue.**

Choose a shape. Cut it in half.
Cut one half in half.
What fraction have you made?
Stick it in your book.

★2 Repeat for other shapes.

A1 Do CM 38.

A2

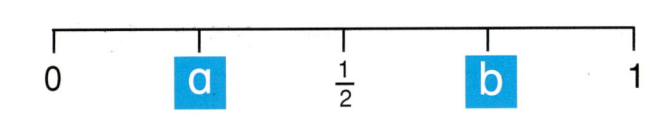

```
|────|────────|────────|────|
0    a       1/2       b    1
```

What are a and b ?

B1 Use this halve-and-halve-again machine to find one quarter of each number.

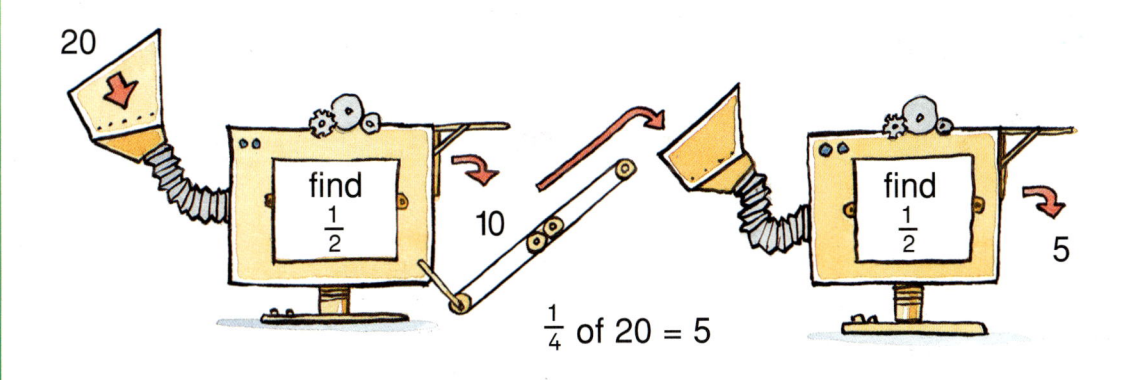

20 → find $\frac{1}{2}$ → 10 → find $\frac{1}{2}$ → 5

$\frac{1}{4}$ of 20 = 5

a 12   b 24   c 40   d 18   e 16
f 8   g 4   h 10   i 80   j 60

F3 Comparing fractions

CM 38

57

F3.2 Number line to 10 (quarters)

Key idea | Fractions are numbers. We can position them on a number line.

B
- Draw each number line.
- Mark the half numbers in red.
- Mark the quarter numbers in blue.
- Answer the questions.

B1

2   3   4

What number is half way between

a 3 and 4?

b $2\frac{1}{2}$ and 3?

c 3 and $3\frac{1}{2}$?

B2

6   7   8

What number is half way between

a 6 and 7?

b 7 and $7\frac{1}{2}$?

c $6\frac{1}{2}$ and 7?

B3

0   1   2   3

What number is half way between

a $\frac{1}{2}$ and 1?

b 1 and 3?

c 0 and $1\frac{1}{2}$?

C1 Draw this number line and put in your own numbers.

Write and answer your own questions.

F3 Comparing fractions

F3.3 Tenths on a number line

Key idea | Knowing that $\frac{5}{10} = \frac{1}{2}$ helps us to compare tenths and one half.

A1 You need 2 packs of digit cards.

Play with a partner.

Shuffle the cards.

Take it in turns to pick a card.

The number tells you how many tenths you have.

If you have more than $\frac{1}{2}$ you win a point.

Return your card to the pack.

First one to 10 points is the winner.

I don't win a point

B1 Look at this number line.

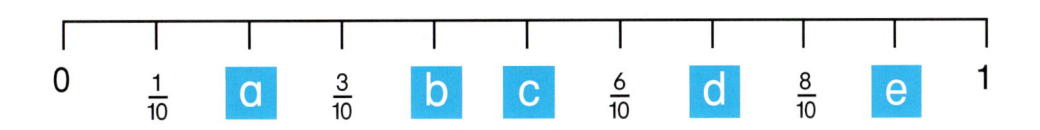

0 — $\frac{1}{10}$ — a — $\frac{3}{10}$ — b — c — $\frac{6}{10}$ — d — $\frac{8}{10}$ — e — 1

What are a, b, c, d and e?

B2 Write down 2 numbers between $\frac{4}{10}$ and $\frac{7}{10}$.

B3 Write down a number that is less than $\frac{6}{10}$ but greater than $\frac{3}{10}$.

F3 Comparing fractions

C Draw each number line in your book.

- Mark $\frac{5}{10}$ numbers in red.
- Mark $\frac{1}{10}$ numbers in blue.

C1

|———————————|———————————|
2　　　　　　　　　　3　　　　　　　　　　4

Write any number between
- **a** $3\frac{1}{2}$ and 4
- **b** 2 and $2\frac{1}{2}$
- **c** 3 and $3\frac{1}{2}$

C2

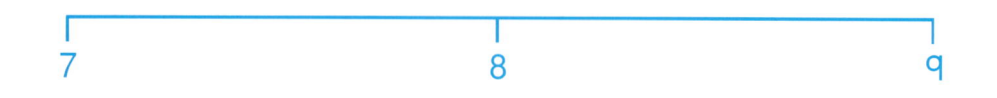

|———————————|———————————|
7　　　　　　　　　　8　　　　　　　　　　9

Write any number between
- **a** $7\frac{1}{2}$ and $8\frac{1}{2}$
- **b** $7\frac{1}{10}$ and $7\frac{1}{2}$
- **c** 8 and 9

C3

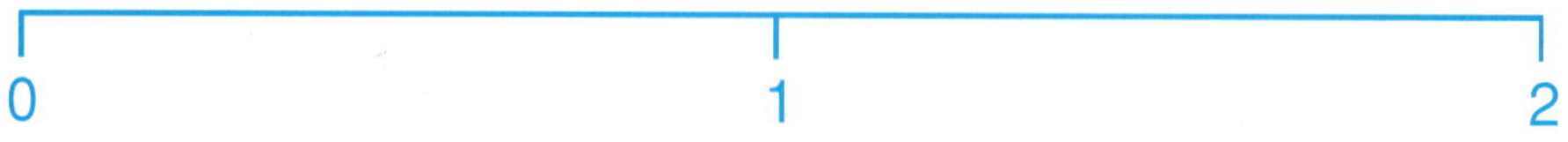

|———————————|———————————|
0　　　　　　　　　　1　　　　　　　　　　2

Write any number between
- **a** 0 and $\frac{1}{2}$
- **b** $\frac{9}{10}$ and $1\frac{1}{2}$
- **c** $1\frac{1}{2}$ and 2

Key idea Knowing that $\frac{5}{10} = \frac{1}{2}$ helps us to compare tenths and one half.

F3 Comparing fractions

F 3.4 Estimating fractions

| Key idea | We can use our knowledge of fractions to estimate fractions of shapes and quantities. |

B1 About what time is it?

a   b   c

B2 The jars hold about 40 gobstoppers when full.
How many are left in each jar now?

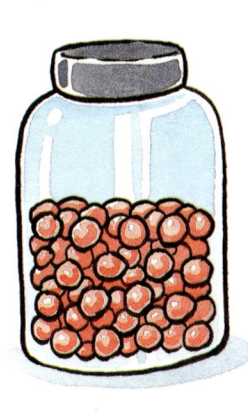

a   b

B3 Draw a number line in your book like this

0   100

a   Mark where half of 100 is. Write in the number.

b   Mark where half of your answer to a is.

C1 Make up 3 of your own estimating fractions questions.

F3 Comparing fractions.

61

F 3.5 Fraction patterns

Key idea | Finding patterns in fractions helps us to solve problems.

★1 a Describe this sequence.

   $0, \frac{1}{2}, 1, 1\frac{1}{2}, 2$

   b What will the next number be?

★2 a Describe this sequence.

   $0, \frac{1}{4}, \frac{2}{4}, \frac{3}{4}, 1, 1\frac{1}{4}$

   b What will the next number be?

A1 Copy this pattern onto squared paper and continue to 5 whole ones.

A2 Continue this pattern to 6.

   $\frac{2}{3}, 1\frac{1}{3}, 2, 2\frac{2}{3}, 3\frac{1}{3},$ _____

A3 The fractions on each ball add up to the number on the seal.
    What is the missing fraction?

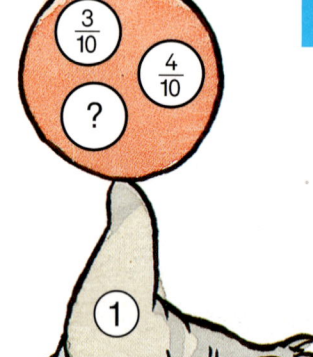

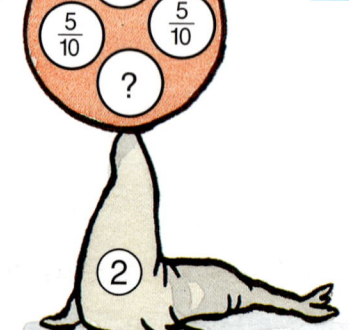

a $\frac{3}{10}$, $\frac{4}{10}$, ? (seal: 1)

b $\frac{5}{10}$, $\frac{5}{10}$, $\frac{5}{10}$, ? (seal: 2)

c $1\frac{3}{10}$, $2\frac{2}{10}$, ? (seal: 4)

62 F3 Comparing fractions

A4 Copy and colour the flags.

a) $\frac{3}{10}$ red
$\frac{5}{10}$ blue
$\frac{2}{10}$ yellow

b) $\frac{1}{10}$ yellow
$\frac{8}{10}$ blue
$\frac{1}{10}$ red

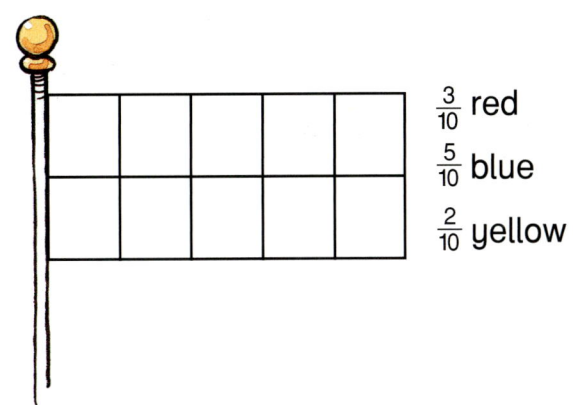

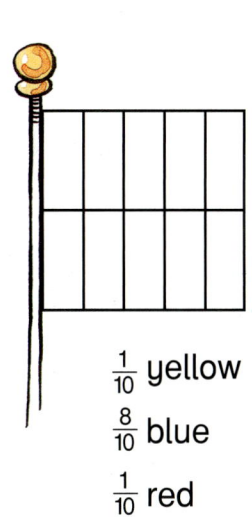

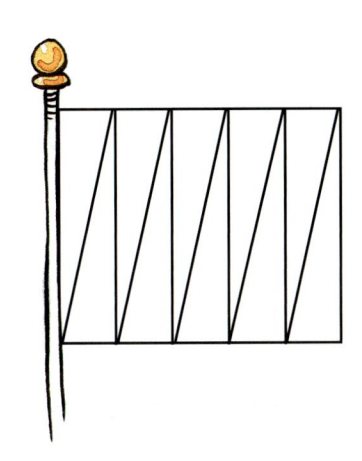

c) $\frac{2}{10}$ yellow $\frac{2}{10}$ green
$\frac{2}{10}$ red $\frac{2}{10}$ white
$\frac{2}{10}$ blue

B1 Even numbers of halves always make whole numbers.

Find 3 examples.

B2 What do you think odd numbers of halves make?

Find 3 examples.

Key idea Finding patterns in fractions helps us to solve problems.

F3 Comparing fractions